Self-Assessment and Goal Setting

Second Edition

By Kathleen Gregory, Caren Cameron, Anne Davies

A Joint Publication

Solution Tree

Connections
Publishing

Published in the US by Solution Tree Press
555 North Morton Street
Bloomington, IN 47404
800.733.6786 (toll free) / 812.336.7700
FAX: 812.336.7790

email: info@solution-tree.com
solution-tree.com

Printed in the United States of America

20 19 18 17 16   3 4 5

FSC
www.fsc.org
MIX
Paper from responsible sources
FSC® C011935

Library of Congress Cataloging-in-Publication Data

Gregory, Kathleen.
  Self-assessment and goal setting / Kathleen Gregory, Caren Cameron, Anne Davies. -- 2nd ed.
      p. cm. -- (Knowing what counts)
  Includes bibliographical references.
  ISBN 978-1-935543-76-3 (perfect bound) -- ISBN 978-1-935543-77-0 (library edition) 1. Students--Self-rating of. 2. Academic achievement. I. Cameron, Caren. II. Davies, Anne, 1955- III. Title.
  LB3051.G725 2011
  371.801'9--dc22
                                          2011008258

Solution Tree
Jeffrey C. Jones, CEO & President

Solution Tree Press
President: Douglas M. Rife
Publisher: Robert D. Clouse
Vice President of Production: Gretchen Knapp
Managing Production Editor: Caroline Wise
Senior Production Editor: Risë Koben

Connections Publishing
Stewart Duncan, CEO & President
Project Manager: Judith Hall-Patch
Design: Karen Armstrong, Mackenzie Duncan, Kelly Giordano, Cori Jones

Acknowledgments

We would like to thank all the students, parents, and educators with whom we have worked. Also, we would like to thank Annalee Greenberg, our editor at A. Greenberg and Associates, for posing thoughtful questions and offering insights.

—Kathleen Gregory, Caren Cameron,
and Anne Davies

Contents

How can I fit self-assessment and goal setting into my already busy schedule? /**59** Students don't take self-assessment seriously; how can I change that? /**59** What is the difference between self-assessment and self-evaluation? /**60** How do you use students' self-assessment information in relation to grades? /**61** Why should I set goals? /**61** What happens if a student's self-assessment is different from my assessment? /**62** Can't I have goals for my students? /**62** Isn't it your job as a teacher to do the assessing? /**63**

Foreword

Where am I going? How am I going? and Where to next? An ideal learning environment or experience occurs when both teachers and students seek answers to each of these questions. Too often, teachers limit students' opportunities to receive information about their performances in relation to any of these questions by assuming that responsibility for the students. . . . Students, too often, view feedback as the responsibility of someone else, usually teachers, whose job it is to provide feedback information by deciding for the students how well they are going, what the goals are, and what to do next. (Hattie & Timperley, 2007, pp. 88, 101)

A formative conception of assessment honors the crucial role of feedback in learning. Research has clearly shown that feedback can promote learning and achievement (Bangert-Drowns, Kulik, Kulik, & Morgan, 1991; Brinko, 1993; Butler & Winne, 1995; Crooks, 1988; Hattie & Timperley, 2007; Shute, 2008), yet most students get little informative feedback on their work (Black & Wiliam, 1998). The scarcity of feedback in most classrooms is due, in large part, to the fact that few teachers have the luxury of regularly responding to each student's work. Fortunately, research also shows that students themselves can be useful sources of feedback via self-assessment (Andrade & Boulay, 2003; Andrade, Du, & Wang, 2008; Ross, Rolheiser, & Hogaboam-Gray, 1999). Self-assessment is a key element in formative assessment because it involves students in thinking about the quality of their own work rather than relying on their teacher as the sole source of evaluative judgments.

Self-assessment is a process of formative assessment during which students reflect on the quality of their work, judge the degree to which it reflects explicitly stated goals or criteria, and revise accordingly. The emphasis here is on the word *formative*: self-assessment is done on drafts of works in progress in order to inform revision and improvement; it is not a matter of having students determining their own grades. Self-evaluation, in contrast, refers to approaches that involve students in grading their work, perhaps as part of their final grade for an assignment or a class. Given what we know about human nature, as well as findings from research regarding students' tendency to inflate self-evaluations when they will count toward formal grades (Boud & Falchikov, 1989), I subscribe to a purely formative type of student self-assessment.

The primary purposes of engaging students in the kinds of thoughtful self-assessment that can be scaffolded using the techniques introduced in this book are to boost learning and achievement, and to promote academic self-regulation, which is the tendency to monitor and manage one's own learning (Pintrich, 2000; Zimmerman & Schunk, 2004). Research suggests that self-regulation and achievement are closely related: students who set goals, make flexible plans to meet them, and monitor their progress tend to learn more and do better in school than students who do not. Self-assessment is a core element of self-regulation because it involves awareness of the goals of a task and checking one's progress toward them—precisely what students do when engaged in the self-assessment and goal setting strategies featured in chapters 1 and 2, respectively. As a result, both self-regulation and achievement can increase (Schunk, 2003).

Although even young students typically are able to think about the quality of their own work, they do not always do so, perhaps because one or more necessary conditions are not present. In order for effective self-assessment to occur, students need to be taught to self-assess and set goals. Goodrich (1996) identified the following elements for success:

- awareness of the value of self-assessment

- access to clear criteria on which to base the assessment

- a specific task or performance to assess

- models of self-assessment

- direct instruction in and assistance with self-assessment

- practice

- cues regarding when it is appropriate to self-assess, and

- opportunities to revise and improve the task or performance

This list of conditions might seem prohibitive but, as this second edition suggests, student self-assessment is both possible and practical. Several of the key conditions listed above, including modeling, cueing, direct instruction, and practice, are commonly employed classroom practices. The second condition—access to clear criteria on which to base self-assessment—can be met by introducing a rubric or checklist (Andrade, 2000; Arter & Chappuis, 2007; Gregory, Cameron, & Davies, 1997; Sadler, 1989).

As this book reveals, there are a number of ways to engage students in effective self-assessment. In general, the process involves the following three steps:

1. *Articulate Expectations.* The expectations for the task or performance are clearly articulated, either by the teacher, by the students, or, preferably, by both together.

2. *Self-Assessment.* Students create first drafts of their assignment and monitor their learning and their progress on the assignment by comparing them to the criteria or rubric.

3. *Revision.* Students use the feedback from their self-assessments to guide revision. This last step is crucial. Students are savvy, and will not self-assess thoughtfully unless they know that their efforts can lead to opportunities to actually make improvements and possibly increase their grades.

This three-step process can be enhanced with peer assessment and teacher feedback, of course. Just these three steps, however, have been associated with significant improvements in students' work (Andrade, 2010).

Students tend to embrace criterion- and rubric-referenced self-assessment for a variety of reasons related to achievement and motivation. In a study of undergraduates, Andrade and Du (2007) report six main findings:

1. Students' attitudes toward self-assessment tended to become more positive as they gained experience with it.

2. Students felt they could self-assess effectively and were more likely to self-assess when they knew what their teacher expected.

3. Self-assessment involved checking progress, followed by revising and reflecting.

4. Students believed there were multiple benefits of self-assessment.

5. Students reported that transfer of the self-

assessment process to other courses, where it was not supported by the instructor, was spotty.

6. There was sometimes a tension between teachers' expectations and students' own standards of quality.

Andrade and Du's (2007) findings generally mirror the results of a study of the impact of teacher professional development on middle and high school students' attitudes toward self-evaluation by Ross, Rolheiser, and Hogaboam-Gray (1998), with one glaring exception: students in the latter study tended to develop more negative attitudes toward self-evaluation over the course of the eight-week intervention. Interestingly, the self-evaluation done by those students counted toward 5% of their final grades. It may not be surprising, then, that students voiced concerns about fairness and the possibility of cheating by inflating self-evaluations. This finding reinforces my commitment to strictly formative uses of student self-assessment.

In summary, blurring the distinction between instruction and assessment through the use of criterion-referenced self-assessment can have powerful effects on learning. The effect can be both short-term, as when self-assessment influences student performance on a particular assignment, as well as long-term, as students become more self-regulated in their learning. I encourage educators to use the strategies in this book to reap the benefits of student goal setting and self-assessment, and thereby ensure that students get the kind of feedback they need, when they need it, in order to learn and achieve.

Heidi Andrade
Associate Professor, Educational Psychology and Methodology
University at Albany, State University of New York

References

Andrade, H. (2010). Students as the definitive source of formative assessment: Academic self-assessment and the self-regulation of learning. In H. Andrade & G. Cizek (Eds.), *Handbook of formative assessment.* New York: Routledge.

Andrade, H. (2000). Using rubrics to promote thinking and learning. *Educational Leadership, 57*(5), 13–18.

Andrade, H. & Boulay, B. (2003). Gender and the role of rubric-referenced self-assessment in learning to write. *Journal of Educational Research, 97*(1), 21–34.

Andrade, H., & Du, Y. (2007). Student responses to criteria-referenced self-assessment. *Assessment and Evaluation in Higher Education, 32*(2), 159–181.

Andrade, H., Du, Y., & Wang, X. (2008). Putting rubrics to the test: The effect of a model, criteria generation, and rubric-referenced self-assessment on elementary school students' writing. *Educational Measurement: Issues and Practices, 27*(2).

Arter, J. & Chappuis, J. (2007). *Creating and recognizing quality rubrics.* Upper Saddle River, NJ: Pearson/Merrill Prentice Hall.

Bangert-Drowns, R. L., Kulik, C. C., Kulik, J. A., & Morgan, M. T. (1991). The instructional effect of feedback in test-like events. *Review of Education Research, 61*(2), 213–238.

Black, P. & Wiliam, D. (1998). Inside the black box: Raising standards through classroom assessment. *Phi Delta Kappan, 80*(2), 139–148.

Boud, D. & Falchikov, N. (1989). Quantitative studies of student self-assessment in higher education: A critical analysis of findings. *Higher Education, 18*, 529–549.

Brinko, L. T. (1993). The practice of giving feedback to improve teaching. *Journal of Higher Education, 64*(5), 574–593.

Butler, D. & Winne, P. (1995). Feedback and self-regulated learning: A theoretical synthesis. *Review of Educational Research, 65*(3), 245–281.

Crooks, T. (1988). The impact of classroom evaluation practices on students. *Review of Educational Research, 58*(4), 438–481.

Goodrich, H. (1996). Student self-assessment: At the intersection of metacognition and authentic assessment. Unpublished doctoral dissertation. Cambridge, MA: Harvard University.

Gregory, K., Cameron, C., & Davies, A. (1997). *Setting and using criteria*. Courtenay, BC: Connections Publishing.

Hattie, J. & Timperley, H. (2007). The power of feedback. *Review of Educational Research, 77*(1), 81–112.

Pintrich, P. (2000). The role of goal orientation in self-regulated learning. In M. Boekaerts, P. Pintrich, & M. Zeidner (Eds.), *Handbook of self-regulation* (pp. 452–502). San Diego: Academic Press.

Ross, J. A., Rolheiser, C., & Hogaboam-Gray, A. (1999). Effects of self-evaluation training on narrative writing. *Assessing Writing, 6*(1), 107–132.

Ross, J. A., Rolheiser, C., & Hogaboam-Gray, A. (1998). Skills-training versus action research in-service: Impact on student attitudes to self-evaluation. *Teaching and Teacher Education, 14*(5), 463–477.

Sadler, D. R. (1989). Formative assessment and the design of instructional systems. *Instructional Science, 18*, 119–144.

Schunk, D. (2003). Self-efficacy for reading and writing: Influence of modeling, goal-setting, and self-evaluation. *Reading & Writing Quarterly, 19*(2), 159–172.

Shute, V. (2008). Focus on formative feedback. *Review of Educational Research, 78*(1), 153–189.

Zimmerman, B. & Schunk, D. (2004). Self-regulating intellectual processes and outcomes: A social cognitive perspective. In D. Dai & R. Sternberg (Eds.), *Motivation, emotion, and cognition: Integrative perspectives on intellectual functioning and development* (pp. 323–349). Mahwah, NJ: Erlbaum.

Introduction

In this book, we show how to involve students in the process of self-assessment and goal setting and provide responses to common questions from students, teachers, and parents. In chapter 1, we provide ten self-assessment activities for students. For each of the activities in this book, we present ways of introducing the idea to students, ways of getting started, and different opportunities for practice. In chapter 2, we describe how to make goal setting a logical extension of self-assessment. In chapter 3, we respond to common questions and concerns.

The examples are given for a specific context or subject area and can be adapted to fit all subject areas. We invite you to select any ideas that interest you and to adapt rather than adopt these to make them work for you and your students.

1. Self-Assessment

What does self-assessment look like?

There are many ways students can assess their own work. Students are involved in self-assessment when, for example, they:

- talk with a teacher about a science project, explaining what it is they are trying to do

- tell a partner how they arrived at an answer in mathematics

- write in a response log at the end of the class, recording key points they have learned and questions they still have

- select, according to criteria, a particular piece of writing to be placed in a portfolio

- summarize in their Spanish quiz book what they need to study for the next quiz

Some self-assessment activities take a few minutes for students to complete while others are more complex and involve a variety of steps. In this book we have organized self-assessment activities under three headings:

- *Pause and Think*. Students assess their work by taking a few minutes to pause and think or reflect about what they are learning.

- *Look for Proof.* Students go one step beyond pause-and-think activities; they select a work sample as proof of an aspect of their learning and comment about their work.

- *Connect to Criteria.* Students assess their work in relation to criteria that have been set for a task or project and find evidence to show they have met the criteria.

How does self-assessment support student learning?

When students assess themselves they *develop insights* into their own learning. Rather than relying on feedback from one person—their teacher—and asking "Is this right?" "Is this long enough?" "Am I doing it right?" and "Is this what you want?" students begin to *monitor* their own learning and consider what part of the assignment meets the criteria and what needs more attention.

When students are involved in self-assessment, they provide themselves with regular and immediate *descriptive feedback* to guide their learning. They become more actively involved in a curriculum that otherwise can seem unrelated to their lives and personal experiences.

How does student self-assessment support teachers?

When students are involved in self-assessment, their teachers can see the gaps between what they have taught and what students have learned. By collecting students' self-assessments, teachers enrich the depth and variety of their data collections about student learning. Teachers go beyond looking at the products and include the students' thinking about their own learning as a key part of their collection of information.

In addition, when teachers provide time for students to assess their own learning on a regular basis, students have time to process new information. Providing time for students to *pause and think*, to *look for proof*, and to *connect to criteria* allows teachers to slow down the pace of their teaching to match the speed of student learning. Students have the opportunity to think about and consolidate their learning before moving on to another topic and covering more curriculum material.

Pause-and-Think activities

In this section, we describe three self-assessment activities that require students to pause and think about their own learning. Each activity is brief, engaging, and requires little teacher preparation. The activities are designed to:

- help students begin to develop skills in thinking about their own learning

- provide teachers with information so they can find any gaps between what has been taught and what has been learned, and

- give students processing time so they can begin to make sense of new material and information

PHRASES AND PROMPTS

Students complete sentence starters that encourage them to think about what they are learning.

Introduce the purpose to students:

> It is important to stop once in a while and pause and think about what you are learning. When you pause and think you give your brain time to process—to make sense—of the new ideas. I am going to set aside time for you to do these activities in class.

The context for this example is watching a video in class.

1. After students have watched a video, record two phrases on the board: "The part I like the best" and "The part I didn't like."

2. Ask volunteers to respond orally to one of these phrases.

3. Have students write responses to one or both phrases in their notebooks.

4. Provide students time to share responses orally with partners.

Provide opportunities for practice:

- Ask students to select phrases from a classroom chart (see figure 1) and use them as sentence starters.

- Have students set up and use a pause-and-think notebook (see figure 2) where they have previously recorded a different prompt on each page. They can select any one of these prompts to respond to when asked.

- Part I liked the best . . .

- What was confusing . . .

- Two things I learned . . .

- One question I have . . .

- I was surprised . . .

- I already knew about . . .

- One thing I know that wasn't mentioned is . . .

- I'd like to know more about . . .

Figure 1: Classroom chart

One thing I want to get better at is...

Some questions I know how to do are...

Some questions I would like to spend more time on...

Pause & Think Notebook

Math

Figure 2: Pause-and-Think notebook

MARGIN SYMBOLS[*]

Students record symbols or phrases in notebook margins to point out to their teacher and to themselves areas they find easy or difficult.

Introduce the purpose to students:

> I need to know what you understand and what you don't so I will know what I need to review and spend more time on in class. To find this out, I am going ask you to record symbols in the margins of your notebooks to let me know what you do well or what you are still not sure about. Taking the time to do margin symbols also helps *you* know where you need to spend your time and energy.

The context for this example is writing a math quiz.

1. On the overhead projector or electronic whiteboard, place a copy of a quiz that students have just completed (but not yet handed in).

2. Tell students that you have made a guess at identifying the three questions you thought would be difficult (D) and three questions you thought would be easy (E). Show students your choices by putting the letters *D* or *E* beside your guesses.

3. Ask students to talk to another person about whether they agree or disagree with your choices.

4. Ask students to record *D* or *E* in the margins on their own quiz beside questions they thought were difficult or easy.

5. Collect the tests and look for patterns from the margin symbols.

6. The next time the class meets, tell students what you learned from their margin symbols and what questions or topics need review.

---

* Adapted from *Thinking in the Classroom*, British Columbia Ministry of Education (1991), Victoria, British Columbia.

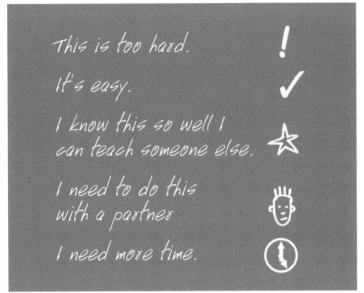

This is too hard.   !

It's easy.   ✓

I know this so well I
can teach someone else.   ☆

I need to do this
with a partner

I need more time.   🕐

Figure 3:
Class margin symbols

Provide opportunities for practice:

- Have students work as a class to develop symbols or phrases that they can use to indicate thoughts about their learning, such as "This is too hard," "It's easy," "I know this so well I can teach someone else," "I need to do this with a partner," or "I need more time" (see figure 3).

- Give students time to complete margin symbols on an outline or overview before they begin a new unit. Then at the end of the unit, have students record new margin symbols using a different color ink to show the change in their learning (see figure 4, page 26).

- Regularly provide time for students to record their thinking in the margins of notebooks, tests, work sheets, and other work. Have students leave their pages with margin symbols open on their desks so you can walk by and see at a glance where students are having difficulty.

New Unit: Poetry

We will be reading and writing diferent forms of poetry
in this unit. Here is a list of what we'll be studying:

Poetic Forms	Beginning of Unit Date: Oct. 15	End of Unit Date: _____
Haiku	✓	
Cinquain	?	
Diamante	?	
Ballad	?	
Limerick	W	
Concrete Poem	W	
Acrostic	☆	
Found Poem	?	
Free Verse	?	
Bio Poem	?	

Key

? I don't know this form.

✓ I've read this before.

W I've written a poem like this.

☆ I like this.

**Figure 4: Margin
symbols for unit**

REFLECTION CARDS

Students reflect on the topic being studied by recording their ideas and questions on a card or piece of paper that can be handed in.

Introduce the purpose to students:

You are asked to think about many different subjects during a school day. You may start thinking about English, then switch to math and then to science—and on and on. Your brain is continually asked to change gears very quickly. To help your brain focus on what we are studying, what your questions are, and what you have learned, I will ask you to record your thinking on "reflection" cards. Sometimes I will give out the cards when we start a class; other times, I will give out the cards during or at the end of class. I will collect these cards, read them, and use the information so I know what to emphasize or to review.

The context for this example is a science lesson.

1. Have students read a section from their text.

2. At the end of the reading, give students a "muddiest point" card (see figure 5). Ask them to write a question about something they don't understand or are not clear on, something that is confusing to them, or something they want more information about.

3. Ask students to put their name on their card if they want an individual response to their question.

4. Collect the "muddiest point" cards.

Figure 5:
Muddiest point card
Reproducible in appendix, page 68

Muddiest Point Card

The muddiest point in *today's class* is: *how do those leaves make the food for the plant?*

Adapted from Angelo & Cross (1993)

5. Take a few minutes after class to sort cards into different types of questions.

6. The next day when the class meets, let students know that the muddiest point cards helped you to determine what they did or did not understand about the section from the text that they read, and proceed with addressing the key questions through discussion, review, or examples.

7. Return cards with a response only to those students who signed their muddiest point.

Provide opportunities for practice:

- Give students a "recall" card when they first enter the class (see figure 6). Ask them to list three points they remember from their last class. As a class, make a collaborative list of what students remember.

Figure 6: Recall card
Figure 7: Exit pass
Reproducibles in appendix, page 68

- Give students an "exit pass" about ten minutes before the end of class (see figure 7). Ask each student to fill in a card and hand it to you as they leave. After class, look for areas of

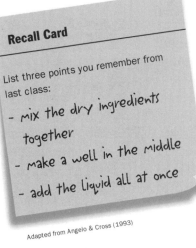

Recall Card

List three points you remember from last class:

- mix the dry ingredients together
- make a well in the middle
- add the liquid all at once

Adapted from Angelo & Cross (1993)

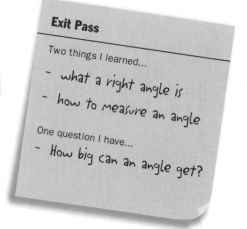

Exit Pass

Two things I learned...

- what a right angle is
- how to measure an angle

One question I have...

- How big can an angle get?

confusion and questions to be addressed during the next class.

- Give students a "one-word web" card at one point during the lesson (for example, part way through a film, after they have completed reading a chapter or a play, after a mini-lesson), and tell them a key word to write in the center of the web. Ask students to web important ideas around this word (see figure 8). Collect the cards to see what students perceive are important ideas around a topic, and use the information to decide what to emphasize or teach again.

- Ask students to record their name on a reflection card only if they have a question they want you to answer privately. Tell them you will write a response on their card for the next class.

Figure 8:
One-word web card
Reproducible in appendix, page 68

Adapted from Angelo & Cross (1993)

Look-for-Proof activities

In this section, we describe three self-assessment activities that go beyond pause-and-think activities by asking students to show proof of their thoughts and ideas. When students find this proof they make their learning *visible* to themselves and others, begin to *show growth* of learning over time, and use this proof as *starting points* for conversations about their learning.

PROOF CARDS

Teachers give students cards that have a word or phrase printed on it—such as "favorite" or "improvement"—that reflects thoughts about a piece of work. Students select an example from their own work that provides evidence or proof of that word or phrase. They then give reasons for their selection.

Introduce the purpose to students:

> It is easy for us to *say* we can do something; it is more difficult to actually *show proof* of what we can do. For example, it is easier to say, "I know how to multiply integers," than it is to prove that you *can* multiply integers. I am going to give you time in class to practice finding proof or evidence of your learning so you and I will both have a clear picture of what you can do.

The context for this example is a French class.

1. Write the following statements on the board:

   the piece that is your <u>favorite</u>

   a piece that you found <u>difficult</u> to do

   something that you and someone else have done successfully <u>together</u>

   one piece that has <u>potential</u>

2. Have students select an example from their own work that illustrates one of the statements on the board.

3. Ask students to share with a partner what they selected.

4. Ask students to record the underlined word (for example, *favorite*, *difficult*, *together*, *potential*) on a piece of paper, attach it to their work sample, and write a reason or reasons for selecting this piece (see figure 9).

5. Ask for volunteers to share an example with the class and tell their reason for selecting it.

Figure 9: Proof card
Reproducible in appendix, page 70

Favorite

This is my favorite because they were fun to write. Please notice the originality of the poems.

Date __Oct. 21__   Signed __Suzanne K.__

Provide opportunities for practice:

- Give students a variety of proof cards to choose from, and encourage them to make up their own (see figure 10, page 32).

- Have students share their work with others, including peers and parents.

- Have students include in their portfolios work samples with proof cards attached.

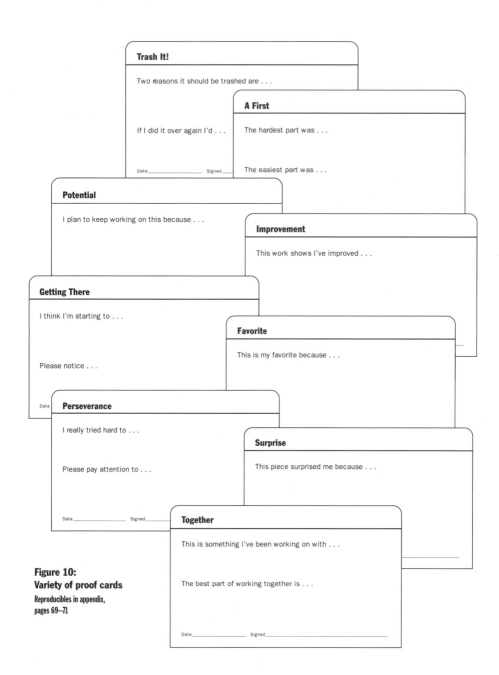

Figure 10:
Variety of proof cards
Reproducibles in appendix,
pages 69–71

BEFORE-AND-AFTER PROOF

Students look at their learning over time by selecting specific examples that show evidence of their growth during the term.

Introduce the purpose to students:

> It is important that you can see improvements that you are making in this class. When you can identify these changes you get to see what you need to continue to do and what you still need to improve. I am going to provide time in class for you to look back at assignments you have completed so you can see how you have improved and notice the areas you still need to work on.

The context for this example is an English class in which students have been writing reader responses since the beginning of the term.

1. Have students select a reader response they completed at the beginning of the term and mark the page with a stick-on note.

2. Ask students to select a second reader response that they have completed recently (one they feel good about), and have them mark the page with a second stick-on note.

3. Have students fill in a "before-and-after" frame (see figure 11).

4. Give students the option to show a partner their before-and-after frame.

Figure 11:
Before-and-after frame
Reproducible in appendix, page 72

| Name ....Date .... |
| I used to: |
| And now I: |

Thanks to Kenneth Koch.

Provide opportunities for practice:

- Give students frequent opportunities to repeat the same type of task during a term or year so they have samples of similar activities to compare (see figure 12).

- Have students make webs at the beginning of a unit to show what they know about a topic before they study it. At the end of the unit, have students add to their web in a different color of ink to show the learning that has taken place since the beginning (see figure 13a).

Name .... Elizabeth W. .... Date .... Jan. 8

Reader Responses

I used to:
- spend my time telling about what happened
- write about 4 lines

And now I:
- write about the characters and what I like about them
- write almost a page

**Figure 12:
Comparing two
reader responses**

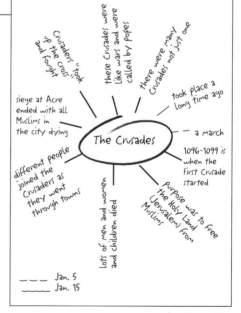

**Figure 13: a)
Student sample
of unit web;
b) Show what
you know
(opposite)**

_ _ _ Jan. 5
_____ Jan. 15

Figure 13a

- Give students a blank sheet of paper (11" x 17") before you begin a new unit of study. Have students sketch, write, or diagram anything they think they already know on the topic. Collect these sheets. Part way through the unit, return the sheets to students and ask them to add information they now know on the topic using a different color of ink. At the end of the unit, repeat the process (see figure 13b).

What I know about fractions

April 17   Fractions are 1/2 1/4 1/10 2/11 5/20ths

This is a fraction →

Pizza pieces are fractions

Fractions can be numbers or words like 1/2, one half, 3/8, three eighths

April 26   Adding up fractions is easy 1/2 + 1/3 and you can subtract too.

1/2 is less than 1 – fractions aren't as big as real numbers.

Improper fractions have the top number that is bigger 20/2

These are the same 1/2 = 2/4

May 5   Fractions can be mixed numbers like 3 1/2 or 1 2/5 and decimals are just like fractions because .5 = 1/2.

When you add or subtract, the bottom of the fraction it has to be the same.

Change to 2/8 = 10/40

+2/10 = 8/40

Now add

May 5.
Please notice I learned to √ and – fractions. Now I know they are like decimals.

Figure 13b

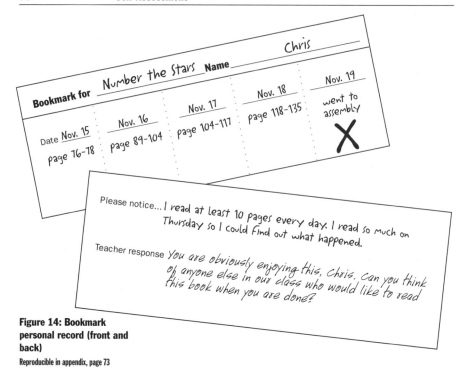

Figure 14: Bookmark
personal record (front and
back)
Reproducible in appendix, page 73

PERSONAL RECORDS

Students keep individual records of what they are doing and learning as a way of showing their improvement and personal growth over time. They use these personal records as evidence of learning.

Introduce the purpose to students:

Many people in sports keep records. Swimmers keep records of their swim times so they can see how they are improving and figure out how they can get even better. Recognizing when you are improving at school helps give you confidence. I am going to give you time in class to keep records that show proof of your learning.

The context for this example is an English class.

1. Provide students with a bookmark on which to record the pages they've read during silent reading time throughout the week.

2. Each day, give students time to record the number of pages they read.

3. At the end of the week, ask students to write a brief comment or comments in the space provided on the reverse of the bookmark.

4. Collect the bookmarks (see figure 14), and write a brief response focusing on individual progress.

5. Continue the process each week to encourage students to get into the habit of keeping personal records.

Provide opportunities for practice:

- Have students keep records of their learning by using graphs, calendar records, or quiz record books (see figures 15a and 15b, page 38).

- Ask students to write summary comments about their learning based on their records.

- Suggest ways that students can share their personal records with others, for example by including them in portfolios and showing them at parent conferences.

Figure 15a:
Quiz record book
Reproducible in appendix, page 74

Quiz Record Book			
Name ___Deanna L.___		Term ___1___	
Subject___French 8___			
Date	Quiz Focus	Score	Comments
Sept. 15	Vocab — transportation	12/15	This was easy.
Sept. 27	er verbs	4/15	I HATE verbs!
Oct. 10	Unit 1	32/40	You didn't tell us that time was on the test

Summary Statement

Signed _____

Date _____

Record of ___The books I read this month___

September

		Bridge to¹ Terabithia (Katherine Patterson)	2	3	4	5
6	7 Dicey's Song (Cynthia Voight)	8	9	Julie of 10 the Wolves (Jean George)	11	12
13	14 Kids Consumer Report Magazine, p. 17—21	15	16 The Egypt Game (Z Snyder)	17	18	19
20	21	22	23 Tire's Burning (J. Lawson)	24 Kids World 10 pages	25	26
27	28	29	30			

Notice that: ___I like fiction best. I don't___
___have a total number of pages but it is___
___about 600 p.___

Figure15b: Calendar record

From Cameron, Tate, Macnaughton, & Politano (1999)

Connect-to-Criteria activities

In this section, we describe self-assessment activities that require students to look at their own performance in relation to criteria. By having criteria for a task or project, students focus on the skills or learning that the criteria describe, think about their own learning *before* they hand work in, and take an active role in the assessment process so they can take more responsibility for their learning.

MET/NOT YET MET

Students assess their work against set criteria and determine whether they have met those criteria or not. Students are prepared to show or talk about the evidence that supports their choice.

Introduce the purpose to students:

> After you complete an assignment, I am going to ask you to look carefully at your work in relation to the criteria and make any changes or additions that are necessary to meet them all. By doing this, you have an opportunity to stop before you hand in your work and see what you have forgotten or what you can improve on.

The context for this example is a writing class.

1. Write the criteria for a descriptive paragraph (previously developed with the class or by the teacher) on the blackboard.

2. Give each pair of students a sample of a descriptive paragraph that meets all criteria (one you have created or an anonymous sample from a previous year).

3. Ask pairs to circle specific evidence of each criterion.

4. Next to the criteria statements, draw two columns on the board.

5. Title one column "met" and the other "not yet met" (see figure 16).

6. Ask volunteers which of the criteria will be checked in "met" or "not yet met" column.

7. The next time the class meets, have students select one of their own descriptive paragraphs.

8. Hand out criteria sheets, with criteria listed opposite "met" and "not yet met" columns (see figure 17).

9. Ask students to circle or highlight specific evidence on their paragraph and put a checkmark in the appropriate column on their criteria sheets.

10. Bring the class together to discuss what they found out about their own writing.

Figure 16: Criteria with Met/Not Yet Met

Criteria for a Descriptive Paragraph	Met	Not Yet Met
- has an introductory sentence		
- uses powerful words that show rather than tell		
- has a concluding sentence		

11. Provide time for students to make changes or additions if they have not yet met the criteria.

12. Ask all students to hand in their paragraphs along with their criteria sheets.

Provide opportunities for practice:

- Give students time in class to work individually or with a partner to check their work against the criteria and to make necessary revisions before they hand in their work.

Criteria for a Descriptive Paragraph	Met	Not Yet Met
- has an introductory sentence		
- uses powerful words that show rather than tell		
- has a concluding sentence		

Date received   Assignment _____

       Student _____

Figure 17: Criteria sheet for students

- After the teacher has assessed student work against the criteria sheets, give students opportunities to resubmit work they have changed or corrected.

- Have students add a third column titled "Please notice" so they can write about special qualities in their work they want their teacher to notice (see figure 18).

Criteria for science lab report	Met	Not Yet Met	Please Notice . . .
- scientific method is complete and easy to follow	✓		I rewrote this twice
- data is accurately presented and interpreted	✓		notice the details in my diagrams and I also included a chart this time
- conclusion(s) is valid	✓		

Conference requested ☑   Question(s):

Date(s) received: Oct. 16   Assignment: Science Lab #4

Assessed by: ☐ teacher ☑ self ☐ partner ☐ other   Student: Aaron D. Block C

Figure 18: Student sample Met/Not Yet Met/Please Notice (science)

SAMPLE MATCH

Teachers post samples of student work (anonymous or teacher-made) such as maps or letters that meet criteria at different levels of quality. Students look at their own work and match it to a sample of work that is the closest match. Students record specific reasons for the match they have made.

Introduce the purpose to students:

> When you are trying to do an assignment and you are not too sure what needs to be included or what it is supposed to look like, it can be very difficult. This is especially true when you have never done a particular task before. To help you see what I expect, I will post samples for some assignments that show different stages of completion and levels of quality.

Figure 19: a) Criteria for map assignment; b) Map sample (opposite)

The context for this example is a social studies class.

1. Show students the criteria for a map (previously developed with the class or by the teacher; see figure 19a).

2. Post two completed samples of a map assignment labeled "sample #1" and "sample #2." These samples may be teacher-made or from a previous year, and they show different stages of completion and levels of quality (see figure 19b).

Criteria for Map	Details/Specifics
- easy to read and follow	- looks good - can read it - uses a ruler to print - it's neat
- labeling is accurate	- correct stuff on it - has title - capital letters used - spelling is correct
- map is complete	- it's colored - put everything on it - shows work - uses a legend - everything is labeled

Figure 19a

3. Point out to students the different levels of quality and completion in the two maps using words and phrases from the criteria.

4. The next day the students meet, have students complete a map assignment, reminding them to keep the criteria and posted samples in mind.

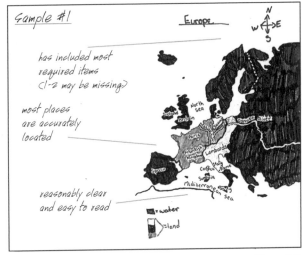

Figure 19b

5. Ask students to take their completed maps and find the sample that it most closely matches. Have them complete the following sentence: "I think my map most closely matches sample X because . . ."

6. Bring the class together and have students discuss questions such as "Was it easy to match your work with a sample? Was it difficult? What are the reasons for your match? What would you need to change on your map to make it match one of the samples?"

7. Give students time to make changes and hand in their map assignments.

Provide opportunities for practice:

- Give students frequent opportunities to match their work with products that have specific formats or components, such as letters, science labs, specific types of paragraphs, steps for solving math problems, or response journals.

PERFORMANCE RUBRIC

Teachers develop a performance rubric that shows different levels of quality for each criterion. Students decide which parts of the rubric provide the closest description of their work or performance.

Introduce the purpose to students:

> Descriptions can help you get a picture of what your work might look like when it is completed. For some of your assignments, I am going to write descriptions for different levels of quality and record them on a rubric. I want you to see which part of the rubric describes your current work, and I also want you to be able to see the next level on the rubric that you are working toward.

The context for this example is group work.

1. Show chart with criteria for group work (previously developed with the class or by the teacher; see figure 20).

2. Provide each group of students with a performance rubric that you have developed for the criteria on group work.

Figure 20: Criteria for group work

Criteria for group work

- get along
- share ideas
- listen to others
- finish the job
- use voices that don't bother others

3. Have students complete a task in their groups, asking them to keep the criteria in mind.

4. Bring the class together, and ask one group to tell where they think their performance fits on the rubric for each criterion. Ask them to provide evidence to support their choices.

5. Have students continue with the group work. At the end of class, ask them to highlight the descriptions that best fit their group's performance (see figure 21, page 46).

Provide opportunities for practice:

- Have students select one criterion on the performance rubric that they could improve.

- Develop three-column performance rubrics for a variety of tasks. Note: We want our students to complete accurate and honest self-assessments. To help them do this, we create performance rubrics using language related to progress, such as *beginning, developing, needs assistance to,* rather than language related to failure, such as *weak, inadequate, undeveloped.*

Criteria for *group work*	**Performance Rubric** 3	2	1
- Get along	enjoyed working together as a team	got along well	most got along with other group members
- Share ideas	everyone contributed	most contributed (some more than others)	some contributed (others needed to be asked)
- Listen to others	all members felt listened to	most group members listened to others	some members needed reminders to listen
- Finish the job	completed all work on time (and thoroughly)	got the job done (may have rushed on parts)	needed more time to finish
- Use voices that don't bother others	consistently used quiet voices	reasonably quiet most of the time	attempted to use quiet voices (needed reminders)

Conference requested ☐

Date(s) received: *Oct. 17*

Assessed by: ☐ teacher ☑ self ☐ partner ☐ other

Question(s): *What one thing would your group need to do differently next time to get the job done?*

Assignment: *Group work on poetry unit*

Student: *Deanna L., Lance G., Mary W.*

Figure 21: Performance rubric completed by group

ACRONYMS

After setting criteria with or for students, teachers decide on an acronym where each letter relates to a criterion statement. For example, BROW stands for "bring a book," "read it," "own it," and "write about it." Students assess their work by recording letters from an acronym that represent the criteria they have met.

Introduce the purpose to students:

> To help us learn, our brain needs to know as soon as possible after doing something how we did. I cannot provide all of you with the immediate feedback you need. One way you can get feedback right away is to use the acronyms based on the criteria we have developed.

The context for this example is partner work.

1. Show students the criteria for partner work (see figure 22).

2. Point out the acronym by circling the letters *T, E, L,* and *L.*

3. Have students complete a partner activity.

4. Invite partners to tell which letters of the acronym they would use to assess how they worked together. Have them give reasons for their decision.

Criteria for Partner Work

Talk about topic

Each person talks

Look at your partner

Listen carefully

Figure 22: Acronym for partner work

Provide opportunities for practice:
- Give students practice in a variety of subject areas (see figures 23a–c).

- Encourage students to create their own acronyms to help them remember what to focus on.

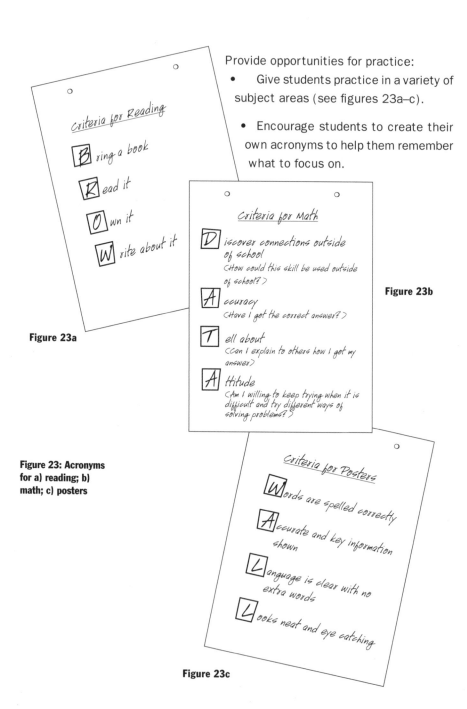

Criteria for Reading

[B] ring a book

[R] ead it

[O] wn it

[W] rite about it

Figure 23a

Criteria for Math

[D] iscover connections outside of school
(How could this skill be used outside of school?)

[A] ccuracy
(Have I got the correct answer?)

[T] ell about
(Can I explain to others how I got my answer)

[A] ttitude
(Am I willing to keep trying when it is difficult and try different ways of solving problems?)

Figure 23b

Figure 23: Acronyms for a) reading; b) math; c) posters

Criteria for Posters

[W] ords are spelled correctly

[A] ccurate and key information shown

[L] anguage is clear with no extra words

[L] ooks neat and eye catching

Figure 23c

2. Goal Setting

What is goal setting?

We see goal setting as a logical next step that follows self-assessment. When students set goals, they decide on something they need to work on and take steps toward achieving that goal. We have students use their self-assessments to decide what they need to work on next. We do not want goal setting to become a separate event that has little connection with what students are doing or that takes up additional class time in an already overloaded schedule.

What are short-term goals?

Short-term goals are small and specific, can be set on a regular basis, and are likely to be achieved within a brief period of time. Following are two methods we use to set these goals.

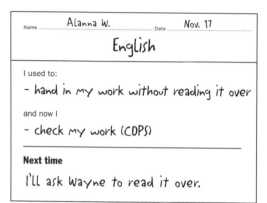

Name .... Alanna W. ....Date........ Nov. 17

English

I used to:

- hand in my work without reading it over

and now I

- check my work (COPS)

Next time

I'll ask Wayne to read it over.

Figure 24a

ADDING A LINE

We have students set short-term goals by using information from their self-assessments to help them decide on their "next step" or goal. We "add a line" to a self-assessment activity so that students see that goal setting is the next step (see figures 24a–c).

Figure 24: a) Add a line to before-and-after frame (above); b) Add a line to proof cards (right and below); c) Add a line to calendar record (opposite)

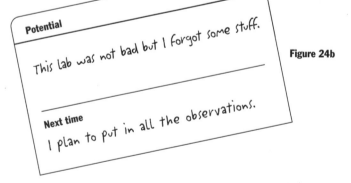

Really tough!

This was really hard for me because I didn't have enough time.

Next time

I plan to ask for more time

Figure 24b

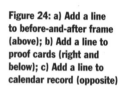

Potential

This lab was not bad but I forgot some stuff.

Next time

I plan to put in all the observations.

Record of ___The books I read this month___

September

		1 Bridge to Terabithia (Katherine Patterson)	2	3	4	5
6	7 Dicey's Song (Cynthia Voight)	8	9	10 Julie of the Wolves (Jean George)	11	12
13	14 Kids Consumer Report Magazine, p. 17—21	15	16 The Egypt Game (Z Snyder)	17	18	19
20	21	22	23 Tire's Burning (J. Lawson)	24 Kids World 10 pages	25	26
27	28	29	30			

Notice that: ___I like fiction best. I don't___
___have a total number of pages but it is___
___about 600 p.___

What's next: ___I'd like to try to get some___
___other books by Julie Lawson.___

Figure 24c

HIGHLIGHTING CRITERIA

When students have criteria for a specific assignment, goal setting can be straightforward. We ask our students to highlight any criterion that they did not meet. This criterion becomes their short-term goal (see figure 25).

Figure 25:
Highlighting criteria

Criteria for Oral Presentation	Details/Specifics
- Interesting to an audience	- look interested in your subject - make it interesting - keep it short
- easy to follow	- use small cards for notes - slow down - use specific examples to get your point across - make sure you have a conclusion - we need to know what your topic is right away
- speech and manner help the audience listen	- look up at your audience - have to be able to hear you - no fidgeting - stand straight

What are long-term goals?

After setting short-term goals, we ask our students to stop and take an overall look at how they are doing in a course, to take stock, and to identify an area they need to focus on to improve. A one- to three-month period gives students a reasonable length of time to make noticeable improvement. The following are three ways to help students set long-term goals:

BREAKING IT DOWN

When we first set long-term goals with our students, we found most set very general goals for themselves. Students had no idea how to begin and often became overwhelmed or confused before they got started. To provide a starting place, we brainstorm lists with our students by answering questions such as "How can we get better at writing?" Making these lists helps to break down general goals into manageable pieces (see figures 26a–e, right and on page 54). Then students select their long-term goals from these lists.

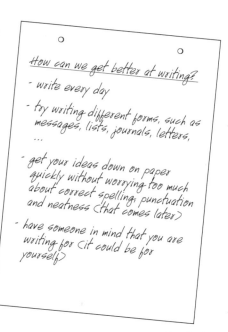

How can we get better at writing?
- write every day
- try writing different forms, such as messages, lists, journals, letters, ...
- get your ideas down on paper quickly without worrying too much about correct spelling, punctuation and neatness (that comes later)
- have someone in mind that you are writing for (it could be for yourself)

Figure 26a: Class brainstorm lists for writing

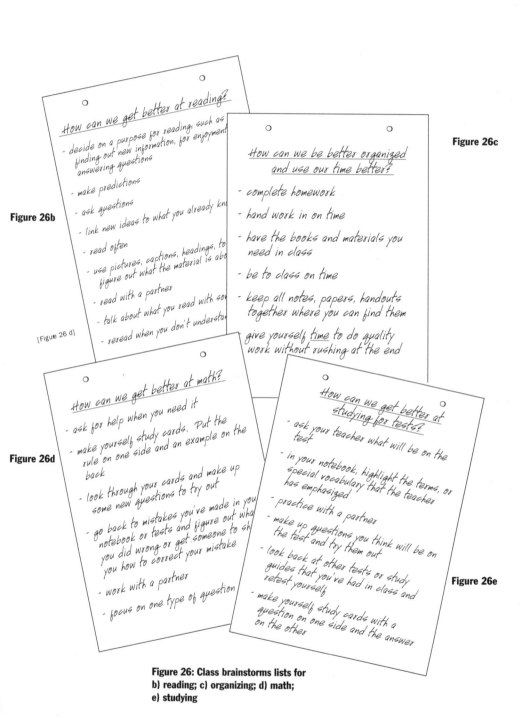

How can we get better at reading?
- decide on a purpose for reading, such as finding out new information, for enjoyment, answering questions
- make predictions
- ask questions
- link new ideas to what you already know
- read often
- use pictures, captions, headings, to figure out what the material is abo
- read with a partner
- talk about what you read with so
- reread when you don't understa

How can we be better organized and use our time better?
- complete homework
- hand work in on time
- have the books and materials you need in class
- be to class on time
- keep all notes, papers, handouts together where you can find them
- give yourself _time_ to do quality work without rushing at the end

How can we get better at math?
- ask for help when you need it
- make yourself study cards. Put the rule on one side and an example on the back
- look through your cards and make up some new questions to try out
- go back to mistakes you've made in you notebook or tests and figure out wha you did wrong or get someone to sh you how to correct your mistake
- work with a partner
- focus on one type of question

How can we get better at studying for tests?
- ask your teacher what will be on the test
- in your notebook, highlight the terms, or special vocabulary that the teacher has emphasized
- practice with a partner
- make up questions you think will be on the test and try them out
- look back at other tests or study guides that you've had in class and retest yourself
- make yourself study cards with a question on one side and the answer on the other

Figure 26b

Figure 26c

[Figue 26 d]

Figure 26d

Figure 26e

**Figure 26: Class brainstorms lists for
b) reading; c) organizing; d) math;
e) studying**

PLANNING FRAMES

We model how to fill out planning frames so students can see how using a frame can help them set long-term goals. Then we help students complete their own individual frames (see figures 27a–d).

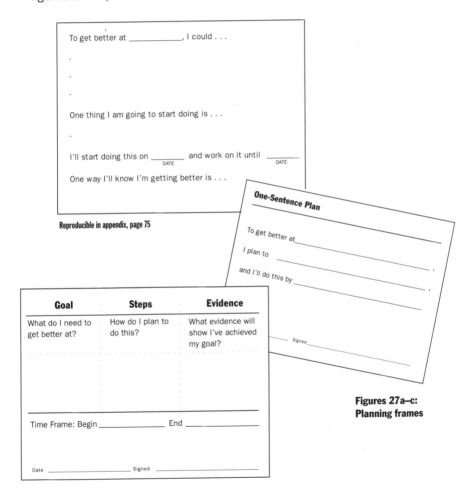

To get better at _____, I could . . .

-

-

-

One thing I am going to start doing is . . .

-

I'll start doing this on _____ and work on it until _____
DATE   DATE

One way I'll know I'm getting better is . . .

Reproducible in appendix, page 75

One-Sentence Plan

To get better at _____

I plan to _____ ,

and I'll do this by _____ ,

_____

Signed _____

Goal	Steps	Evidence
What do I need to get better at?	How do I plan to do this?	What evidence will show I've achieved my goal?

Time Frame: Begin _____ End _____

Date _____ Signed _____

Figures 27a–c: Planning frames

Picture

What is your overall goal?

What do you want to be able to do?

Piece

What specific part of the goal will you start with?

Plan

How will you get there?

How long will it take?

Partner

Who will support you and keep you moving forward?

Perform

Show what you can do now that you couldn't do before.

From Cameron, Tate, Macnaughton, & Politano (1999)

Figure 27d: Planning frame

ASKING QUESTIONS

We have found that when students work with others to clarify, refine, and monitor their long-term goals, they are more likely to see value in the process of goal-setting. We provide class time at various times during the goal setting process for students to have a peer interview (see figure 28), have a teacher interview (see figure 29, page 58), and complete a student self-review of their goal plans (see figure 30, page 58).

Peer Interview

- Is your goal possible?

- Is the time frame reasonable?

- What will others notice when you are improving? (e.g., parents, friends, teacher)

- What will you be able to show/tell others as proof that you are working on your goal?

- Who do you think could help you achieve this goal?

Figure 28: Peer interview questions

Teacher Interview

How are you doing with your goal so far?

Do you need to make any changes? e.g., time frame
                                        goal itself
                                        steps

How can I help you?

Figure 29: Teacher interview questions

Student Self-Review

What did I learn by working toward my goal?

What was the biggest obstacle?

What was the biggest help along the way?

Figure 30: Student self-review
Reproducible in appendix, page 76

3. Questions and Responses

Q. Self-assessment and goal setting take time. How can I fit this into my already busy schedule?
(teacher)

R. Self-assessment and goal setting *do* take time. Teachers who use class time to teach students the skills of self-assessment and goal setting believe this is time well spent because students learn to identify their own strengths, needs, and what they need to work on next. As a result, their learning improves. For us, involving students in self-assessment and goal setting has become an integral part of our instruction, not an add-on.

Q. I tried having students assess their own work, but they didn't take it seriously; they just wrote anything. How can I change that? (teacher)

R. Students need to learn not just how to assess their learning—they need to know *why,* and *how* it is going to help them. Teachers need to model the process and work through examples, help students develop the vocabulary of self-assessment, and let them know what is expected of them. When students can see how self-assessment and goal setting connect to what they are learning and how their teacher is using their self-assessment information, they become more committed and skilled.

Q. What is the difference between self-assessment and self-evaluation? (teacher)

R. Assessment and evaluation have different meanings and purposes. Assessment involves collecting information on student performance; evaluation involves examining all of the assessment data and then making judgments about individual performance. We use the term *self-assessment* because we want students to think about and collect information on their own learning—not make judgments. When students assess their own work, they describe their learning, match it to work samples, use rubrics, and see how it relates to criteria. We do not ask our students to evaluate their work by giving themselves numbers, percentages, or grades. These kinds of judgments actually get in the way of learning, because students focus on the number or grade and rank themselves in relation to other students rather than focus on their own specific learning or progress. Learning is enhanced when students see their strengths, understand what they need to work on, and are able to set personal goals. For these reasons, we now ask students to assess and not evaluate their own work.

Q. How do you use students' self-assessment information in relation to grades? (administrator)

R. The information that students collect about their own learning provides just one component of the data we use in evaluation. We also collect a variety of products that students complete, our observations of their skill development and performances, as well as information from our conferences and interviews. When we examine all of this information, including self-assessment information, we can get a more complete picture on which to base our evaluations. We want students to be involved in self-assessment so they can collect information on their own learning. It is our job to evaluate—to use all of the assessment information (including students' self-assessments) to make judgments on individual performance and, if required, give grades.

Q. Why should I set goals? I can't learn it anyway. (student)

R. This question and statement illustrate a critical issue, particularly among middle and secondary students, about students' beliefs concerning their own learning. We found we have to step back and work with our students to help them understand some truths about learning. Their beliefs were often based on the idea that a person is born "smart," "dumb," or "in the middle." They did not believe that improved effort, better organizational skills, more time spent on assignments, or specifically focusing on one or two skills could make any difference to their learning. We work with our students to help them see how certain actions could improve their learning. We talk about how people learn in different ways and in their own time. Without taking the time to discuss the beliefs about learning that our students bring to class with them, some students will see goal setting as yet one more thing over which they have no control.

Q. What happens if a student's self-assessment is different from my assessment? (teacher)

R. When students write a self-assessment that is significantly different from our assessment, we ask for a brief conference. Teachers might say, "I am interested in seeing the evidence you have to show proof of your assessment," or "Tell me about your reasons for this assessment." A conference gives both teachers and students new insights and opportunities to clear up any areas of confusion.

Q. Are the students the only ones who set goals? Can't I have goals for them? (teacher)

R. For years, we set goals for our students. A statement such as "Jeremy needs to spend more time completing his homework and reading more at home at night in order to improve" is an example. However, for many students and parents such a statement was simply a line on the report card: there was no monitoring, no follow-up, and no recognition of accomplishment. When we asked students about goals we had set for them, they didn't remember the goal, didn't understand it, or had no idea how to achieve it—there was no ownership and no motivation. Today we involve our students in goal setting because it leads to ownership—students are more likely to "buy in." We've also learned that we best use our time when we teach our students the skills they need to set appropriate goals for themselves.

Q. **My son tells me he assesses his own work. Isn't it your job as a teacher to be doing the assessing?**
(parent)

R. We *do* assess students' work by collecting a variety of information on what individuals know, where there are gaps in the learning, and what they need to work on next. In addition, we ask students to assess many of their assignments, as numerous research studies make it clear that when students are involved in self-assessment, their achievement improves. One major study (Black & Wiliam, 1998a) points out that to improve achievement, "pupils should be trained in self-assessment so that they can understand the main purposes of their learning and thereby grasp what they need to do to achieve" (p. 10). The study also states that involving students in self-assessment results in improved learning for all students, particularly those who struggle the most. As we want to make sure students have the best possible opportunity for learning, we involve them in self-assessment activities on a regular basis. Evaluation, on the other hand, differs from assessment, as it involves making overall judgments about how well students are achieving—this remains the responsibility of the teacher.

Conclusion

When we involve students in self-assessment and goal setting, they develop insights about their own learning and learn to give themselves specific, descriptive feedback, which is essential for learning. What counts for us is that we involve students in self-assessment and goal setting as a way of supporting the learning of all of our students.

Self-Assessment and Goal Setting is the second book in the *Knowing What Counts* series, three books in which we describe ways of involving students in all aspects of assessment. The series also includes *Setting and Using Criteria* (book 1) and *Conferencing and Reporting* (book 3). The focus for each book is on classroom assessment practices that support learning for all students.

Appendix: Reproducibles

Note: The following pages may be reproduced for classroom use. To enlarge to working size, set photocopier at 133 percent, and align top edge of pages with corresponding edge of copier glass.

Muddiest Point Card

The muddiest point in _____

is:

Recall Card

List three points you remember from last class:

-

-

-

Exit Pass

Two things I learned . . .

-

-

One question I have . . .

-

One-word web card

Trash It!

Two reasons it should be trashed are . . .

If I did it over again I'd . . .

Date_____ Signed_____

A First

The hardest part was . . .

The easiest part was . . .

Date_____ Signed_____

Potential

I plan to keep working on this because . . .

Date_____ Signed_____

Self-Assessment and Goal Setting, 2nd Edition, by K. Gregory, C. Cameron, and A. Davies
© 2000, 2011 • solution-tree.com

Improvement

This work shows I've improved . . .

Date_____ Signed_____

Getting There

I think I'm starting to . . .

Please notice . . .

Date_____ Signed_____

Favorite

This is my favorite because . . .

Date_____ Signed_____

Perseverance

I really tried hard to . . .

Please pay attention to . . .

Date_____ Signed_____

Surprise

This piece surprised me because . . .

Date_____ Signed_____

Together

This is something I've been working on with . . .

The best part of working together is . . .

Date_____ Signed_____

Self-Assessment and Goal Setting, 2nd Edition, by K. Gregory, C. Cameron, and A. Davies
© 2000, 2011 • solution-tree.com

Name .... Date ....

I used to:

And now I:

Bookmark for _____ **Name** _____

Date _____

Please notice . . . .

Teacher response

Self-Assessment and Goal Setting, 2nd Edition, by K. Gregory, C. Cameron, and A. Davies
© 2000, 2011 • solution-tree.com

Quiz Record Book

Name_____   Term _____

Subject _____

Date	Quiz Focus	Score	Comments

Summary Statement

Signed _____

Date _____

Self-Assessment and Goal Setting, 2nd Edition, by K. Gregory, C. Cameron, and A. Davies
© 2000, 2011 • solution-tree.com

To get better at _____, I could . . .

–

–   –   –

One thing I am going to start doing is . . .

–

I'll start doing this on _____ and work on it until _____
                            DATE   DATE

One way I'll know I'm getting better is . . .

Self-Assessment and Goal Setting, 2nd Edition, by K. Gregory, C. Cameron, and A. Davies
© 2000, 2011 • solution-tree.com

Student Self-Review

What did I learn by working toward my goal?

What was the biggest obstacle?

What was the biggest help along the way?

Self-Assessment and Goal Setting, 2nd Edition, by K. Gregory, C. Cameron, and A. Davies
© 2000, 2011 • solution-tree.com

Bibliography

Angelo, T. A. & K. P. Cross. 1993. *Classroom Assessment Techniques: A Handbook for College Teachers* (2nd Edition). San Francisco: Jossey-Bass Publishers.

Black, P. & D. William. 1998a. Assessment and classroom learning. *Assessment in Education, 5*(1), 7–75.

Black, P. & D. William. 1998b. Inside the black box: Raising standards through classroom assessment. *Phi Delta Kappan, 80*(2), 137–148.

Cameron, C., B. Tate, D. Macnaughton, & C. Politano. 1999. *Recognition Without Rewards.* Winnipeg, MB: Peguis Publishers.

Gregory, K., C. Cameron, & A. Davies. 2011. *Setting and Using Criteria* (2nd Edition). Bloomington, IN: Solution Tree Press.

Preece, A. 1995. Involving students in self-evaluation. In A. Costa and B. Kallick, *Assessment in the Learning Organization.* Alexandria, VA: Association for Supervision and Curriculum Development.

Stiggins, R. 1996. *Student-Centered Classroom Assessment* (2nd Edition). Columbus, OH: Merrill Publishing.

Kathleen Gregory, BA, MEd, has more than 30 years' experience teaching at secondary, elementary, and middle schools. With a background in assessment practices and literacy strategies, she has also been a district curriculum coordinator and a support teacher for classroom teachers and school teams who are integrating students with special needs. A former teacher-in-residence at the University of Victoria, Kathleen is currently an instructor for literacy and assessment courses for pre-service teachers and is a consultant to many school districts in developing their own approaches to conferencing, reporting, and authentic assessment strategies.

Caren Cameron, MEd, has worked as a teacher, a District Principal of Educational Programs, and a sessional instructor at the University of Victoria. Currently she is an educational consultant working with school districts across Canada on a variety of topics including assessment and leadership. She is the co-author of a dozen practical books for colleagues, including a series for middle and primary years called *Voices of Experience*.

Anne Davies, PhD, is a researcher, writer, and consultant. She has been a teacher, school administrator, and system leader, and has taught at universities in Canada and the United States. She is a published author of more than 30 books and multi-media resources, as well as numerous chapters and articles. She is author or co-author of the best-selling books *Making Classroom Assessment Work*, the *Knowing What Counts* series, and the *Leaders Series*. A recipient of the Hilroy Fellowship for Innovative Teaching, Anne continues to support others to learn more about assessment in the service of learning and learners.